A Zondervan/Ladybird Bible Book

Jesus the Child

By Jenny Robertson
Illustrated by Alan Parry

ZONDERVAN
PUBLISHING HOUSE
OF THE ZONDERVAN CORPORATION
GRAND RAPIDS, MICHIGAN 49506

Beans and yellow peas bubbled in the pot. Mary was mixing dough to make bread when a voice called her. She looked up, amazed, and saw a stranger with a light shining from his face. "The Lord is with you, Mary," he said. "He is pleased with you. God will give you a baby boy whose name is to be Jesus. He is the Son of God, the promised King who will save His people."

At first Mary was puzzled. Then she said, "I am the Lord's servant maid. I will do whatever he says."

3

"People said such unkind things when they heard you would have a baby soon," Joseph the carpenter remembered. "At first I thought we should not marry."

"I know," Mary said. "Then God showed you in a dream what to do. You believed him and married me."

Their goats played beside them and Mary fondled the wiggling kid. "Shall we start our journey to Bethlehem before my baby is born?" she asked.

"I am afraid we must pack our things and set off very soon. The Romans, who rule our country, want everyone to travel to the place where he was born. We will be registered, counted, and taxed. It will be a hard journey for you. Bethlehem is a long way from here."

"God will look after us," Mary reminded Joseph.

"We are nearly at Bethlehem now!" Joseph encouraged Mary.

"I'm glad!" she said. "We've slept outside so often, with only a little fire to keep wild beasts away. It will be safer in the yard of an inn with other people. I shall be glad to lie down! My baby will be born soon."

"King David herded his father's sheep on these very hills," said Joseph. "Our teachers say that Bethlehem, King David's town, will be the place where the promised King will be born."

"Hurry, little donkey!" said Mary. "The teachers told the truth! Our baby King will be born in royal Bethlehem!"

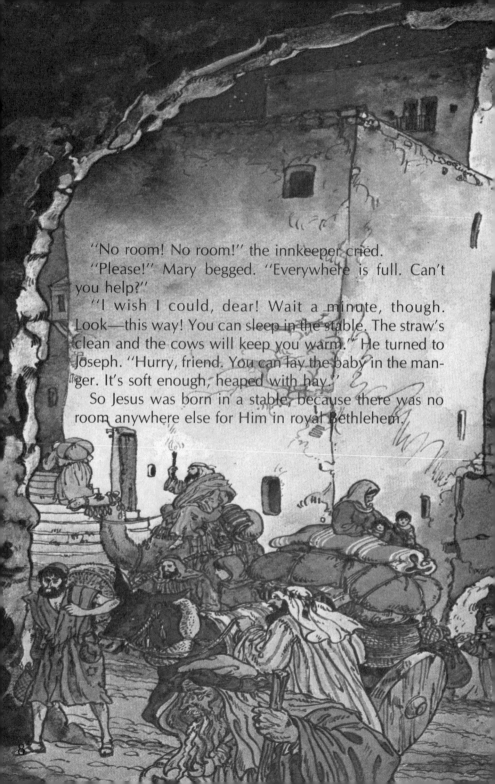

"No room! No room!" the innkeeper cried.

"Please!" Mary begged. "Everywhere is full. Can't you help?"

"I wish I could, dear! Wait a minute, though. Look—this way! You can sleep in the stable. The straw's clean and the cows will keep you warm." He turned to Joseph. "Hurry, friend. You can lay the baby in the manger. It's soft enough, heaped with hay."

So Jesus was born in a stable, because there was no room anywhere else for Him in royal Bethlehem.

"News, good news for everyone!" Hundreds of shining messen-gers, brighter than the starlit sky, looked down at the terrified shepherds. "Don't be afraid," said one of the angels. "Your prom-ised King, your Savior, has been born. He is close by, in Bethlehem, a baby wrapped in linen cloth, lying in a manger. Go quickly and see." Then the angels sang, "Glory, glory to the most high God. Peace to His people on earth."

"We came as soon as we heard the news. We left our sheep. The Lord God will guard them from harm."

Trying to tiptoe, the shepherds crowded into the stable and knelt beside the manger where Jesus slept on the hay.

"Oh, praise God! Thank God! He has sent this little one to be our Savior. The promised King is born in a stable, not in a king's great palace. God has not forgotten us, His poor people."

Telling everyone the news, the shepherds hurried away, while Mary sat and watched her baby boy.

"It's dark in the stable," Mary said. "The cows low and stamp. Rats run about in the hay, but the music of highest heaven plays for You, dear Jesus. Sleep well, little one. Sleep well."

Wise men came riding toward Bethlehem. Each dry, hot day they rested, shaded by their kneeling camels. At night they rode on. The cold wind stung their faces.

"The star told me a King is born. I am old, yet when I saw the star I left my home and my books to follow it."

"Surely we shall find the baby at the royal palace! The star told me the newborn child is to be a King of wonder, who will rule forever."

The king, Herod, welcomed the wise men, but their news worried him.

"A star told these visitors that a wonderful King is born in *my* kingdom!" Herod thought. "Where is this promised King to be born?" he asked the priests.

"In Bethlehem, O king!" The priests bowed, hating their ruler who did not know the promises of God.

"I must get rid of this baby!" Herod decided to himself. "*I* am king in this land."

"Search for the child in Bethlehem," Herod told the wise men. "Tell me where to find Him. I wish to bow before Him also," he lied.

The wise men found Mary and Jesus in a house in Bethlehem.

"Here is gold for the King of Kings," said one.

"I have brought sweet-smelling frankincense. I worship God in this small child," another said, bowing low.

"Little King, I give You myrrh, for You will heal many hurts, though this will do You harm," said a third.

"I heard the sound of children crying as we left Bethlehem," Mary said.

"I heard that sound, too, in my sleep last night," Joseph said. "God warned me of terrible danger. Herod plans to kill our baby King. He is sure to send his soldiers after us if he discovers we have gone."

"Where will we be safe?" Mary asked.

"God told me to take you and Jesus far away to another country, to Egypt. We will make our home there until God tells us it is safe to return. Many of our own Jewish people live in Egypt. We are sure to find friends."

So the little family lived happily in Egypt until it was safe for them to go home to Nazareth.

"That's fine, Jesus," said Joseph. "Pull that end away now!" Jesus saw His mother and called, "Our door is nearly ready!" Mary smiled at her son. He was growing up so sturdy and strong. No one here in little Nazareth knew about the star, or the wise men with their costly gifts.

When Jesus was twelve years old, he traveled to Jerusalem with His parents and other families. It was wonderful to climb up to the golden Temple! Long after the other families from Nazareth left, Jesus stayed.

"Who is this boy?" the teachers and priests wondered. "He knows the writings that tell of God's promises, but even more, He knows God Himself in a special way."

"Jesus!" Joseph tiptoed in. "Your mother and I have searched for you for two days!"

"Why have you done this to us?" Mary asked.

"Did you not know I must learn My Father's ways?" Jesus answered. But He went quietly home with Mary and Joseph.

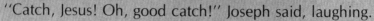

"Catch, Jesus! Oh, good catch!" Joseph said, laughing.

"May I play, too?" Daniel asked.

"Of course! We're on our way to Capernaum, where I often do repairs for the fishermen. And Jesus likes to help."

"We see my cousins, too," Jesus said. "Catch, Daniel!"

Mary wondered if it had all been a dream—the splendid messenger who told her the news about her child; the excited shepherds who praised God for sending the promised King; the wise men who bowed before her baby; the escape into Egypt. They were such an ordinary family! Yet she knew that one day Jesus would put away His carpenter's tools and do the work God His Father planned: bringing the love of God to everyone.

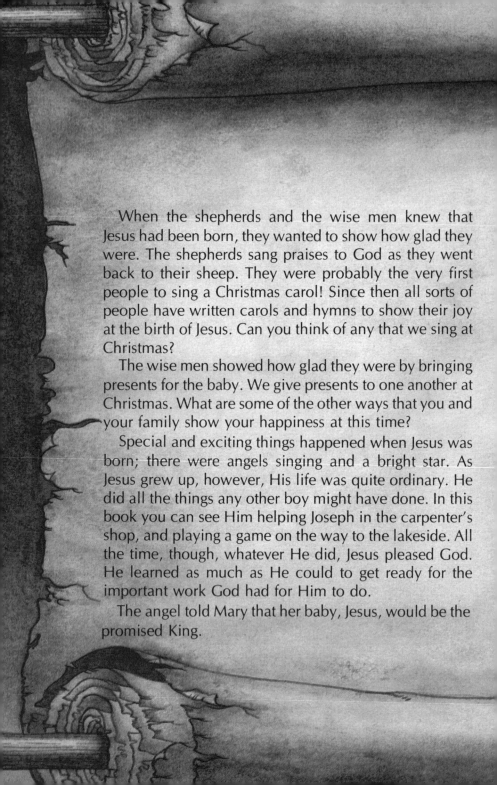

When the shepherds and the wise men knew that Jesus had been born, they wanted to show how glad they were. The shepherds sang praises to God as they went back to their sheep. They were probably the very first people to sing a Christmas carol! Since then all sorts of people have written carols and hymns to show their joy at the birth of Jesus. Can you think of any that we sing at Christmas?

The wise men showed how glad they were by bringing presents for the baby. We give presents to one another at Christmas. What are some of the other ways that you and your family show your happiness at this time?

Special and exciting things happened when Jesus was born; there were angels singing and a bright star. As Jesus grew up, however, His life was quite ordinary. He did all the things any other boy might have done. In this book you can see Him helping Joseph in the carpenter's shop, and playing a game on the way to the lakeside. All the time, though, whatever He did, Jesus pleased God. He learned as much as He could to get ready for the important work God had for Him to do.

The angel told Mary that her baby, Jesus, would be the promised King.